A Special Gift For:

_____

From:

_____

When:

_____

*May you know the sweet joy of intimacy
with the One you were made for.*

Praying you hear the sweet
voice of your Savior.

Conversations
with God

---

40 Days of
Intimate Reflection

by Kelley Latta

About the Author

Kelley Latta is a Bible teacher, event speaker, and writer who has a passion for teaching believers how to approach Christ through His Word to live transformed lives.

Having professed faith in Jesus as a child, Kelley was confronted in her mid-twenties by the reality that her beliefs about Christianity didn't match up with Jesus' teachings. Compelled into the Word to discover Truth for herself, she encountered Jesus through its pages and finally experienced the transforming power of grace. She now aims to help the body realize the saving reality of authentic intimacy with Jesus Christ.

Kelley serves Hanover First Church of God in Hanover, Pennsylvania as a member of the Heart to Heart Women's Ministry team. She teaches a women's class on Sunday mornings and often leads a weekly Bible study. Kelley answered God's call to full-time service in July of 2011 with the launch of Kelley Latta Ministries.

Along with her weekly online post, "Kelley's Word on Wednesday," Kelley is the author of *Tested by Fire*, an interactive Bible study that guides readers into discovering their God-given purpose. She also travels with Strive for Greatness' Women of Purpose Conferences as one of their featured speakers.

In 1994, Kelley married her best friend, Steve. Together they find great joy in serving the Lord and raising their two amazing sons, Austin and Mason.

Introduction

40 Days in His Presence

Psalm 31:15 states, *"My times are in your hands."* Do you believe that to be true? Do you know that God chose you to dwell in this time and this place because He has a great purpose for you to fulfill? He has, dear one, and He's ready to do something extraordinary through you.

You hold this journal by divine invitation. Your Creator invites you into sweet fellowship and godly purpose, and He awaits your response. He's not seeking a body to fulfill a duty. No, He searches for a heart ready to respond to the revelation of His will.

You see, prayers that open the floodgates of heaven find their source in God Himself. Jesus taught us that principle when the Disciples asked Him to teach them to pray. After exalting and worshiping the name of the Father, Jesus spoke these words to His eager students:

"Your kingdom come, your will be done on earth as it is in heaven."
Matthew 6:10

God's perfect will has been set forth in the heavens. Ephesians 1:3 teaches that we have *already* been blessed in the *heavenly realms* with every spiritual blessing available to us in Jesus. Our role is to cooperate with Him to call those blessings down. To do so, we must quiet ourselves to listen so that He can reveal it to us.

"Be still, and know that I am God; I will be exalted among the nations, I will be exalted in the earth." **Psalm 46:10**

This prayer journal offers 40 days of Scripture and reflection to help guide you into the practice of relationship with your Maker. Why does relationship matter? Because God desires to know you and be known.

*"Now this is eternal life: **that they may know you**, the only true God, and Jesus Christ, whom you have sent."* **John 17:3**

Do you know God and the Son that He sent? Do you want to?

Before Jesus began His earthly ministry, He spent 40 days in the desert with nothing but the Spirit and the Word to sustain Him. There Satan tempted Him, yet He emerged victorious and sinless, combating him with Scripture and drawing on the power of the Spirit. He returned from that time empowered to begin His ministry, and the world was forever changed.

How will God empower you in these next 40 days?

I'm so thankful you've decided to join me on this journey. As you meet with God each day, I encourage you to quiet your heart before Him and invite Him to speak His thoughts to you before you offer your words to Him in prayer. His words, after all, hold the power.

Blessings, dear one. His glorious purpose waits to be revealed. May He enthrall you with the joy of discovery, and may your brush with Glory leave you changed.

Praying you hear the whisper of God,

Kelley

Day 1: Powerful Words

> "So is my word that goes out from my mouth:
> It will not return to me empty, but will accomplish what I desire and
> achieve the purpose for which I sent it." **Isaiah 55:11**

God's voice cut through the darkness, "Let there be . . ." And there *was*. I wonder if a hush fell over heaven as the angels readied themselves to hear God speak. I imagine they gazed intently into the darkness, poised to witness life bursting forth at the mere sound of the Creator's voice. However they began, what they saw compelled them to erupt in worship,

> " . . . *the morning stars sang together and all the angels
> shouted for joy."* **Job 38:7**

Once again God stands ready to speak, anxious to whisper His desires into the hearts of those children who have tuned their ears to hear. His words still carry the power to create, but He no longer directs them toward a vast expanse of darkness. Now He speaks to His created. *He speaks to you.*

We serve a God who *"calls things that are not as though they were"* (Romans 4:17), and that's what they become. Are you ready to hear what He's saying to you?

Do you believe God speaks? Do you believe His words still hold the power to create life where it did not exist? Do you believe they can change you?

Prepare your heart by quieting your mind and focusing your thoughts on the Lord. Ask God to speak to you now, opening your heart to receive

His words to you. Write the thoughts He gives you on the lines below, and offer your response to Him in prayer.

_____

_____

_____

_____

_____

_____

_____

_____

_____

_____

_____

_____

_____

_____

_____

_____

_____

_____

_____

Day 2: Made to Hear Him

... He wakens me morning by morning, wakens my ear to listen like one being taught. Isaiah 50:4

God created you to hear Him. In fact, before sin entered the picture, God walked among His creation and conversed with those He made.

Everything changed, however, the moment man chose to ignore the warnings of his Creator and take from the forbidden tree. Sin severed the sweet fellowship that had existed between God and man, its presence within Adam's heart denying communion with God's perfect holiness. Immediately, unfamiliar emotions like fear, loss and shame took hold of Adam, causing him to hide from the Lord.

Then the man and his wife heard the sound of the Lord God as he was walking in the garden in the cool of the day, and they hid from the Lord God among the trees of the garden. But the Lord God called to the man, "Where are you?" **Genesis 3:8-9**

I love God's heart revealed in this verse. Even when we make destructive choices—when we disobey, run from God, or push Him away—He still pursues us. His heart aches over our separation and He calls us to Him. He also makes a way for us to draw near.

The Lord God made garments of skin for Adam and his wife and clothed them. **Genesis 3:21**

At the time of man's first sin, God covered Adam's shame through sacrifice: He shed the blood of innocent animals to atone for Adam's sin and restore his ability to meet with God.

A greater sacrifice has been given for you. The blood of God's own Son poured out from a cross, not just to cover your sin, but also to release you from its destructive pull. If you desire to abandon your sin and believe in Jesus' ability to cleanse you by His sacrifice, He will provide you access into God's presence. Your ability for intimate fellowship with God has been restored. All that remains is for you to choose it.

Do you desire fellowship with your Creator, dear one? Are you tired of sin's destructive presence in your life? Will you believe that Jesus made the way to be free? Offer a prayer of surrender on the lines below. Confess your sin and invite Jesus to come dwell within you and change your heart. Commit to follow Him, choosing each day to listen for the voice of His Spirit. Thank Him for His sacrifice.

_____

_____

_____

_____

_____

_____

_____

_____

_____

_____

_____

_____

_____

_____

Day 3: The Word is Near

"The word is near you; it is in your mouth and in your heart,"
that is, the word of faith we are proclaiming.

Romans 10:8

Sweet, intimate fellowship with humanity has always been the central desire fueling God's heart. Distance does not satisfy Him. He wants to draw near.

Consider His history. He enjoyed unfettered communion with Adam and Eve at creation and sought to preserve that relationship by keeping them from sin. When they chose to disobey and broke fellowship with Him, He called a nation out from this world to be His own, teaching them His ways so that He could dwell among them. When they stumbled and rejected Him, He sent His Son as a love offering, that all people might respond to His invitation to know Him.

"I revealed myself to those who did not ask for me;
I was found by those who did not seek me.
To a nation that did not call on my name,
I said, 'Here am I, here am I.'"
Isaiah 65:1

Having done all that, do you think He's keeping His distance from you?

Dear one, God desires to reveal Himself to you personally. The Word has come. His Spirit is near, speaking words of truth that hold the power to transform your heart and life. Will you tune your ear to hear Him?

Do you experience God's nearness? Are you aware of His presence whispering words of life into your heart? He is with you right now, beckoning you to notice Him. Quiet yourself and invite Him to make Himself known to you. Take some time to journal any thoughts He gives you. Ask Him to help you become more aware of Him so that you can truly know the God who is near.

_____

_____

_____

_____

_____

_____

_____

_____

_____

_____

_____

_____

_____

_____

_____

_____

_____

_____

Day 4: A Private Tutor

The unfolding of your words gives light; it gives understanding
to the simple. Psalm 119:130

I used to find God's Word difficult to understand, so I relied on Bible teachers and pastors to explain it to me. I rarely opened my Bible except for Sundays. I had no idea what I was missing.

Can you relate? Does the prospect of studying Scripture seem burdensome? Do you assume it's beyond your ability to understand?

You're right, of course. Quite frankly, it's beyond your pastor's ability. Even the Disciples, who had Jesus for a teacher, needed divine intervention to truly understand the Bible.

Then he opened their minds so they could understand the Scriptures.
Luke 24:45

Thankfully, God hasn't left us relying on ourselves to understand His Word. He sent us an interpreter.

*What we have received is not the spirit of the world, but the Spirit who is from God, **so that we may understand** what God has freely given us.*
1 Corinthians 2:12

If you belong to Jesus, the One who dwells within you isn't limited by your intellect or education. He simply requires your time and a listening heart. He longs to perform the task in your life that God sent Him to do. He wants you to understand what you've been given, and He's ready to teach you. You just need to offer Him a teachable heart.

12

"But the Counselor, the Holy Spirit, whom the Father will send in my name, will teach you all things and will remind you of everything I have said to you." **John 14:26**

Are you ready to let the Counselor teach you? Spend some quiet time in prayer asking God to search your heart. What's keeping you from meeting with Him in His Word? Invite Him to reveal Himself to you and teach you His ways. Then commit to follow.

_____

_____

_____

_____

_____

_____

_____

_____

_____

_____

_____

_____

_____

_____

_____

_____

_____

Day 5: Uncontainable

> " ... The heavens, even the highest heaven, cannot contain you.
> How much less this temple I have built!"
>
> **1 Kings 8:27**

We spend a lot of time telling God how He should be. We tell Him what we want from Him; then we refuse to forgive Him when He doesn't meet our expectations. We believe we should be able to explain Him, so we make Him fit an idea we can understand. Then we set limits on what we'll expect from Him so we won't end up disappointed.

Essentially, we'd like God to behave. As long as He remains within the boundaries we've established for Him, we'll believe. So we spend our lives trying to contain an uncontainable God. Then we resent Him for not showing up when we need Him.

> *You turn things upside down, as if the potter were thought to be like the clay! Shall what is formed say to him who formed it, "He did not make me"?* **Isaiah 29:16**

We began as dust resting upon the surface of the ground. God scraped His hands across the earth He had made, gathering that dust to Himself. Then He lovingly formed a man from what He held and *"breathed into his nostrils the breath of life"* (Genesis 1:26). Only then did man become a living being.

We have no right to attempt to shape God to fit the limits of our understanding. It's time to release him from the temples we have built and worship Him as He is. *Uncontainable. Untamable. Perfect. Sovereign.*

Have you unknowingly tried to shape God to fit into a mold you have made? Will you open your mind to the possibility that the God of Scripture far surpasses the boundaries of the temple you've built to house Him?

Take some time to consider your own view of God, writing your beliefs on the lines below. Ask Him to show you where you've placed limits on Him and help you release any misconceptions. Offer a prayer relinquishing your ideas to the Lord and invite Him to show you who He really is.

_____

_____

_____

_____

_____

_____

_____

_____

_____

_____

_____

_____

_____

_____

_____

Day 6: The Lord of Glory

He wraps himself in light as with a garment; he stretches out
the heavens like a tent and lays the beams of his upper chambers
on their waters. He makes the clouds his chariot
and rides on the wings of the wind.

Psalm 104:2-3

Scripture paints an awesome picture of our great God. Encased in light, He fills the heavens and soars upon the clouds. Magnificent, glorious, powerful . . . He rides on the wings of the wind. How could we ever know a God who remains at such lofty heights?

Ah, but He didn't remain there, beloved. He descended to the earth to call all people to Him. As He did, Jesus chose to do something even more shocking. He left behind His majesty to become like you and me.

*Who, being in very nature God, did not consider equality with God
something to be grasped, but made himself nothing, taking the very
nature of a servant . . . And being found in appearance as a man, he
humbled himself and became obedient to death — even death on a cross!*
Philippians 2:6-8

Why would He do such a thing? Why would the Lord of glory choose to offer Himself as a sacrificial lamb? Psalm 18:35 says it best, *" . . . you stoop down to make me great."*

Jesus humbled Himself so that He could exalt *us*. He descended to raise us to our fullest potential. He died so we could become all He created us to be. He lives so we can fellowship with Him forever.

16

Jesus exchanged His nature for yours so that He could save you from yourself. He asks that you follow His example. Will you exchange your nature for His?

Contemplate the reality that Jesus "stooped down to make you great." Write what you think that means for you on the lines below and offer Him a prayer of gratitude.

_____

_____

_____

_____

_____

_____

_____

_____

_____

_____

_____

_____

_____

_____

_____

_____

_____

Day 7: The Proper Response

"Woe to me!" I cried. "I am ruined! For I am a man of unclean lips, and I live among a people of unclean lips, and my eyes have seen the King, the Lord Almighty." **Isaiah 6:5**

The prophet Isaiah enjoyed the remarkable privilege of seeing God's glory revealed in His temple. One response overpowered all else at the revelation: sheer terror.

What brought on his despair? He became acutely aware of his own depravity for the very first time. God's perfect holiness laid bare his own impurity, washing it in righteous light. He realized this Supreme Being had every right to smite him, and he declared himself ruined.

No wonder Scripture repeatedly teaches,

> *"The fear of the LORD is the beginning of wisdom, and knowledge of the Holy One is understanding."* **Proverbs 9:10**

Fear of God marks the beginning of our journey toward redemption. Without it, we can't fully comprehend God's mercy and grace. Do you fear Him, dear one?

I confess that for a long time, I didn't. I heard so much about God's grace and forgiveness that I couldn't wrap my brain around the thought that I should fear Him. It didn't compute with the image I had been given. I was told God was my friend.

As a result, I had a carefree attitude toward sin. I didn't think it mattered much. After all, grace covers it, right?

Perhaps this is one reason why much of Christ's church looks so little like Him today. Salvation doesn't begin with grace; it ends there. Salvation *begins* with fear.

Do you possess the fear of the Lord? Have you drawn near to His presence and allowed Him to reveal His true nature to you? Have you responded to Him with sorrow over your sin?

Meditate on what you think it means to fear God. Ask Him to show you whether you approach Him with a proper reverence for His holiness or if you've made Him out to be something less than He is. Confess what He shows you below and ask Him to expand your view of Him.

_____

_____

_____

_____

_____

_____

_____

_____

_____

_____

_____

_____

_____

_____

Day 8: Moved by fear

The fear of the Lord is the beginning of knowledge, but
fools despise wisdom and discipline. **Proverbs 1:7**

Our journey with God must begin with humble, awed reverence for who He is. Until we truly recognize the height of our depravity and our desperate need of Him, we won't reach out for salvation. We'll continue to overlook our sin and believe we're capable of making something of ourselves. That's what Jesus meant in **Matthew 5:3** when He said,

"Blessed are the poor in spirit, for theirs is the kingdom of heaven."

What type of fear does your heart hold toward God? Do you shrink back at the thought of trusting Him, convinced that He will take more from you than He will ever give? Or do you have an awe of God that causes you to approach Him in an attempt to know Him more?

Abraham had the kind of fear that propelled Him toward God. **Acts 7:2-4** tells us,

"The God of glory appeared to our father Abraham while he was still in Mesopotamia, before he lived in Haran. 'Leave your country and your people,' God said, 'and go to the land I will show you.' So he left . . ."

At the beckoning of God, Abraham left his people and his home to go to a land he'd never seen. Why would he do that? How could he so easily and completely abandon everything to follow this God?

In the midst of a polytheistic culture that offered its worship to many gods, Abraham met the God of glory. Truth penetrated his heart, and he

20

knew this was the One True God.

Imagine the magnitude of the encounter; it convinced him that all he had ever been taught to believe was wrong. Abraham beheld something awesome that conceived in Him the fear of the Lord. Yet this fear did not send him running to the hills. It sent him chasing after this God he realized he simply could not live without. Abraham's fear of remaining distant from God surpassed his fear of approaching Him. He was compelled to follow, and the path led him straight into God's blessing.

Has your knowledge of God sent you chasing after Him, or have you remained in the same place you were when you began? Do you believe you're better off keeping your distance from God? If so, why? Ask Him to show you whether you possess a godly fear or whether fear is keeping you from His blessing. Journal your thoughts, and commit to follow Him.

_____

_____

_____

_____

_____

_____

_____

_____

_____

_____

_____

_____

_____

Day 9: Great Reward

> After this, the word of the LORD came to Abram [later named Abraham] in a vision: "Do not be afraid, Abram. I am your shield, your very great reward." **Genesis 15:1**

We get excited about reward. We often spend our lives striving after it in some way or another. Whether the compensation we seek resembles the love of a child, the attention of a spouse, recognition at work, or monetary gain, we often find the satisfaction we get upon achieving our goal less fulfilling than we thought it would be.

God made a profound statement to Abraham, the man He chose to become the father of His great nation. He announced plainly, "I am your reward."

I wonder how long it took Abraham to believe Him.

Think about it. Would you believe Him? Do you today?

Consider the rewards fixed in your own gaze. Is God among them? If not, you're not alone. For many, God serves as the means to an end, not the end goal itself. We view God as a method to obtain what we really seek—security, blessing, the promise of heaven—but most of us can't comprehend the idea that He might actually *be* the reward.

And so we ask God to provide the things we believe will satisfy us and ignore the only thing that will: God Himself.

Would you open your mind to consider that God spoke a revolutionary truth to Abraham in Genesis 15:1? This verse holds the secret to finally abiding in joy, living at peace, and becoming a beneficiary of God's promises. Will you consider believing that God Himself **is** *"your very great reward,"* far surpassing the things you've been striving after?

What reward do you seek, dear one? What do you hope to gain by drawing nearer to God? Ask God to show you whether He is the source of your delight or the means to another perceived blessing. Write what God reveals to you on the lines below. Ask Him to shift your desires toward Him rather than what you think He can give you.

_____

_____

_____

_____

_____

_____

_____

_____

_____

_____

_____

_____

_____

_____

_____

_____

_____

Day 10: Saved by Knowing

"Now this is eternal life: that they may know you, the only true
God, and Jesus Christ, whom you have sent."
John 17:3

Most of us get it wrong. We can't fathom a God who created the whole
world caring about the likes of us, so we set about living our lives
without caring much about the likes of Him.

Yet something within us senses we aren't alone in the universe, so we
determine to find some sort of religion that meets our interests, satisfies
our needs and appeases the Higher Power. But we won't let it consume
us. We'll just meet the minimum requirements as we understand them
and hope it's enough.

Yet Scripture teaches that only one thing will be enough to attain eternal
life in heaven: knowing the God who created you by following the Son
He sent.

> *Jesus answered, "I am the way and the truth and the life. No one
> comes to the Father except through me."* **John 14:6**

Acts 4:12 adds,

> *Salvation is found in no one else, for there is no other name under
> heaven given to men by which we must be saved.*

One name holds the power to save, and that's Jesus. Yet attending a
Christian church, celebrating Christmas and Easter, knowing a lot about

Jesus, or even doing works in His name won't buy you entrance into the heavenly city of gold.

In fact, tickets can't be purchased at all. Rather, Jesus seeks an offering, given in response to His great gift of love poured out on the cross. Jesus merely asks for your heart.

Have you trusted Jesus with your heart? Do you know Him personally and intimately, or have you substituted knowing about Him for real relationship? Ask Him to help you describe your current relationship with Him and journal your thoughts below. Pray that He would give you a desire to draw near to Him and follow where He leads.

_____

_____

_____

_____

_____

_____

_____

_____

_____

_____

_____

_____

_____

_____

_____

Day 11: Love's Revelation

"Whoever has my commands and obeys them, he is the one who loves me. He who loves me will be loved by my Father, and I too will love him and show myself to him."

John 14:21

My life changed forever in response to these four words: Do you love Jesus?

I can honestly say I thought I did. I interpreted the warm feeling of joy in my heart during Sunday morning worship as love. I didn't realize it was my soul rejoicing as it joined creation in doing what God created us to do.

Then our pursuing God showed me the truth of what was in my heart one day as I worked through a Bible study: "You do not love me." I remember the shocking realization settling in, the nearness of God's presence refusing to allow me to deny the truth any longer. I had been a pretender, living a lie.

The moment marked a turning point. I could have chosen to keep going through the motions of church, living my version of Christianity. No one would've known except God and me.

Instead, I fell to my knees, broken before the Lord who died to save me, and confessed my sin. Then I asked Him to teach me to love Him, and I discovered the marvelous truth of John 14:21. A heart poured out before the Lord of glory that is set on loving Him through dedicated obedience enjoys a remarkable privilege. Jesus begins to show Himself.

Have you been going through the motions with God? Is your relationship marked by duty or loving intimacy? Do you see Jesus revealing Himself in your life?

Open your heart to the Spirit of God and ask Him to show you the truth about your own walk with Him. Do you love Him? Journal your thoughts and confess anything God reveals. Ask Jesus to teach you to love Him so He can show Himself in your life.

_____

_____

_____

_____

_____

_____

_____

_____

_____

_____

_____

_____

_____

_____

_____

Day 12: He Will be Found

"You will seek me and find me when you seek me with all your heart."
Jeremiah 29:13

Have you ever watched a toddler chasing his daddy? Picture the scene.

On wobbling legs, he gleefully scampers in pursuit, fully believing he's in control of the game. His father glances over his shoulder to see how close he's getting, eyes twinkling. But before the little one can grab hold of his elusive daddy, his father turns and scoops him up, laughingly wrapping him in his embrace. Suddenly the pursuer finds himself caught by the one he pursued.

I imagine our heavenly Father feels the same kind of glee when we seek Him. Yet He only allows us the joy of discovery when He knows our hearts are in it.

Jeremiah 29:13 teaches that we must search wholeheartedly to find God. We won't stumble upon Him with careless thoughts or half-hearted desires.

But for the heart that longs for its Creator and seeks to discover truth, **Jeremiah 29:14** adds this promise,

"I will be found by you," declares the Lord, "and will bring you back from captivity."

God takes the burden of finding Him off of us and places it upon Himself. If we truly desire to find Him, we don't ever have to worry that we'll miss Him. He will make sure He is found. Like the daddy who surprises his little child by turning toward him and catching him, your heavenly Father will scoop you into His arms when you least expect it. And both of you will erupt with joy.

Have you been caught by your heavenly Father? Has God "made himself found" to you? Ask him to show you what has hold of your heart that's keeping you from discovering Him personally and journal your thoughts on the lines below. Invite Him to set your heart fully on Him.

_____

_____

_____

_____

_____

_____

_____

_____

_____

_____

_____

_____

_____

_____

_____

_____

_____

Day 13: In This Generation

From one man he made every nation of men, that they should inhabit the whole earth; and he determined the times set for them and the exact places where they should live. **Acts 17:26**

Contrary to what you may believe about yourself, you were no accident. And your presence in this time and this place isn't happenstance. You are here by divine design.

Has it occurred to you that your life holds great significance to your Creator? That you are cherished, sought after, and created with purpose?

If you hesitate to believe that, consider Scripture's explanation of why God determined your particular time and place.

God did this so that men would seek him and perhaps reach out for him and find him, though he is not far from each one of us. **Acts 17:27**

God set you in this time and within your individual circumstances so that you *"would seek him and perhaps reach out for him and find him."*

What does that do to your soul, dear one? To know that God chose your particular circumstances because within them you would be more inclined to seek and know Him?

Have you allowed your situation to turn your heart to the Lord?

Take a moment to contemplate God's love and pursuit of you. Ask Him to reveal Himself to you in a fresh new way. Invite Him to show you something new about His purpose and presence in your circumstances.

Write your thoughts on the lines below, and offer back a prayer of gratitude for His divine intervention in your life.

_____

_____

_____

_____

_____

_____

_____

_____

_____

_____

_____

_____

_____

_____

_____

_____

_____

_____

_____

_____

Day 14: I AM

God said to Moses, "I AM WHO I AM. This is what you are to say to the Israelites: 'I AM has sent me to you.'"

Exodus 3:14

Have you encountered I AM? I have. His revelation in my life brought me to my knees. Now He waits to show Himself to you.

Each time God reveals one of His names in Scripture, He teaches an attribute of His character. The name reveals a way that He desires for us to experience Him.

I AM is one of my favorites. Each time He speaks it, He reminds us to trust in who He is. When we can't make sense of our circumstances, He whispers, "I AM." When we face the impossible and there seems to be no way, He boldly claims, "I AM." When all seems lost and the enemy *looks* victorious, God still IS.

On the night of Jesus' arrest, an angry mob carrying torches and weapons approached Him and His Disciples in an olive grove. When they claimed to be looking for Jesus of Nazareth, Jesus answered, "I am he."

The next moment defied all reason.

> *When Jesus said, "I am he," they drew back and fell to the ground.*
> **John 18:6**

Jesus never raised a weapon. He merely stated who He was, and the weapon bearing soldiers collapsed. In that moment, God made flesh declared Himself by His covenant name,

I AM WHO I AM.

And His enemies could not stand.

Have you trusted God to reveal who He IS in your life? Have you given Him opportunity to prove that His plan for you has little to do with who you are and everything to do with who He is? Ask God to show you where you've trusted what you see instead of who He is. Journal what He reveals and ask Him to help you surrender.

_____

_____

_____

_____

_____

_____

_____

_____

_____

_____

_____

_____

_____

_____

_____

_____

_____

_____

_____

Day 15: Foolish Things

But God chose the foolish things of the world to shame the wise;
God chose the weak things of the world to shame the strong.
1 Corinthians 1:27

God delights in you. Wherever you've come from, however you see yourself, God sees something wonderful. He sees the person He made you to be. What do you see?

Perhaps you see weakness. God sees an opportunity to show His strength. That happens to be His specialty. In fact, He chooses the weak so He has greater opportunity to reveal Himself.

Consider Paul's words to the Corinthian church.

Brothers, think of what you were when you were called.
Not many of you were wise by human standards; not many were
influential; not many were of noble birth. But God chose the foolish
things of the world to shame the wise . . .
1 Corinthians 1:26-27

If you see yourself as not having the proper credentials for God to do something with your life, then you're a perfect candidate for glory.

He chose the lowly things of this world and the despised things—and the
things that are not—to nullify the things that are, so that no one may
boast before him. (**Verses 28-29**)

Our confidence in our own abilities interferes with God's work. Pride stops the flow of God's power into our lives; it takes our gaze off of God and shifts it back on us. Yet when we allow God to give us an accurate picture of what we are **not** and choose to trust Him to use those things for His glory, we open the door to the revelation of His power.

How do you view yourself? Do you imagine you're too weak . . . that you're not smart enough . . . that you're nobody special? Ask God to show you who He sees. Jot down what you consider your areas of greatest weakness and surrender them to God for His use. Invite Him to become your strength and reveal Himself through your limitations.

Day 16: The Will to Follow

"My sheep listen to my voice; I know them, and they follow me."
John 10:27

Follow through. Have you ever noticed how our intentions rarely make it to reality? Dreams remain just that. Goals change and resolutions dissolve, rising and falling with the whim of our current desires. And let's face it; our desires change as quickly as our moods.

We need a constant. A truth and a way that holds us steady so we don't veer off course and self-destruct, a light to illuminate our path and guide us into fulfilling our true desires.

You know the ones, even if you can't name them. They're the source of your restlessness, your purpose and gifts woven into the fabric of who you are and camouflaged by your deceitful heart (Jeremiah 17:9).

You aimlessly wander from one idea to the next trying to satisfy their call, but you never will. Not without the One who placed them within you when He made you.

Jesus answered, "I am the way and the truth and the life."
John 14:6

Jesus is the Way to quiet the restlessness. He alone holds the Truth of who you really are and what you were made to do. He is the only path to experiencing the fullness of Life on earth and eternal life in heaven. And He beckons you toward glory with two words. *"Follow me."*

Do you believe Jesus holds the key to finding true contentment and purpose? Will you trust Him with your daily choices and give Him the right to lead? Ask God to help you surrender your desires to Him. Allow Him to show you what's keeping you from following His plan and write what you hear. Then invite Him to lead.

_____

_____

_____

_____

_____

_____

_____

_____

_____

_____

_____

_____

_____

_____

_____

_____

_____

Day 17: A Freewill Offering

I will sacrifice a freewill offering to you; I will praise your name,
O LORD, for it is good. **Psalm 54:6**

We wander aimlessly along paths of our own choosing, hoping to stumble upon abundant life. Like blind sheep we stray from its true source, not realizing we avoid the sheltering protection of our Shepherd to our detriment. Our insistence to go our own way leads to destruction.

Yet the Shepherd still honors our right to choose. Unlike our enemy, He doesn't seek slaves. Rather, He looks for souls who will open their hearts to love Him. He searches for individuals who will submit their wills freely to His because they trust Him, and they recognize his worth.

It is written: "'As surely as I live,' says the Lord, 'every knee will bow before me; every tongue will confess to God.'" **Romans 14:11**

One day God will remove our freedom to choose. One glorious, dreadful day all will finally be disclosed and Jesus will claim His throne. Knees will fall to the earth in trembling awe. Some consumed by fear because they did not choose it. Others weeping with joy at the sight of their Savior, confident in their position because the posture is familiar. They chose to bend their knees to His will while He still offered a choice.

What will that day hold for you, dear one? Will fear grip your heart, or will you experience consuming joy? Your outcome that day rests with you. Today, He still offers the right to choose.

Have you offered yourself to the Lord, committing to bow to His will? Is He Lord and Master of your steps? Ask Him to reveal the depth of your commitment to Him. Journal your thoughts and invite Him to help you surrender wholeheartedly to His will.

_____

_____

_____

_____

_____

_____

_____

_____

_____

_____

_____

_____

_____

_____

_____

_____

_____

_____

_____

_____

_____

_____

Day 18: Saving Your Soul

> Therefore, putting aside all filthiness and *all* that remains of wickedness, in humility receive the word implanted, which is able to save your souls. **James 1:21, NASB**

Jesus gave up His life to save you . . . to *ransom your soul*. Have you ever stopped to consider what that really means?

Three parts of you comprise your soul: your mind, your will and your emotions. Your thoughts, desires and feelings combine to make up who you are. Under the nurturing leadership of your Creator, these three echo His loving character and propel you toward abundant life.

But the soul of man didn't remain under God's loving care. Man's choice to sin entangled our hearts with evil and bound our souls in slavery to darkness. Our thoughts, desires and feelings now lead us down the path of self-destruction.

Without Jesus' intervention, we cannot trust our deceiving minds. Action taken in fear proves folly. Doubt paralyzes us into missed opportunity. Worldly logic defies God's plans and tricks us out of His blessings.

Our feelings also betray us. We instinctively follow our hearts with abandon, unaware that *"The heart is more deceitful than all else and is desperately sick . . . "* (Jeremiah 17:9, NASB)

Like powerful magnets, our desires draw us toward those things that are most harmful to us. Even the foods we choose to eat reflect the destructive nature of our will. We blindly follow the longings of our sin nature, discovering too late the consequences of our allegiance.

Jesus descended from on high to rescue your soul from darkness. He offers to restore dominion over your thoughts, desires, and feelings. Will you allow Him to save your soul?

Does logic hinder your ability to trust? Do you wrestle with fear and doubt? Against ungodly desires? Ask God to show you where He longs to set you free, and write it below. Invite Him to take control of you. Commit to give Him all of you—body and soul. Then follow Him to redemption.

_____

_____

_____

_____

_____

_____

_____

_____

_____

_____

_____

_____

_____

_____

_____

_____

Day 19: Behind the Veil

And we, who with unveiled faces all reflect the Lord's glory,
are being transformed into his likeness with ever-increasing glory,
which comes from the Lord, who is the Spirit.

2 Corinthians 3:18

I spent most of my life hiding. I didn't like who I was, so I pretended to be someone else.

My family loved me very much, but something inside me could never believe it. I always felt *less than*, so I tried to compensate by being good. Not just good, actually, I strove to excel. Unfortunately, that striving didn't win me any popularity contests in school. Very quickly, I learned to wear a mask.

Then I carried that mask into my marriage. I wore it in church. I even hid behind it from my friends and family members. It became so much a part of me I didn't recognize it as a mask. Even I believed the lie.

I'm so grateful for the promise of **2 Corinthians 3:16**.

But whenever anyone turns to the Lord, the veil is taken away.

When Jesus intersected my path and revealed my need to love Him, His light began to penetrate my life. I started to recognize my insecurities and believe I could be different. Then suddenly, I was.

I didn't need to keep thinking the same destructive thoughts; Jesus gave me new truths to focus on. I didn't need to put up walls and keep people at a distance; I was safe with Him. I learned to trust because the object of my trust was now fully trustworthy, and as I began to trust Him, Jesus taught me how to love.

And when we love, dear one, we reflect the true image of God.

Have you drawn near to Jesus and allowed Him to lift the veil in your life? Ask Him to show you what's hiding behind your veil. As He reveals your areas of hurt and brokenness, write down what He shows you and offer those things back to Him to redeem. Then celebrate as He begins to transform your heart.

_____

_____

_____

_____

_____

_____

_____

_____

_____

_____

_____

_____

_____

_____

_____

_____

_____

Day 20: From the Inside Out

Surely you desire truth in the inner parts;
you teach me wisdom in the inmost place. **Psalm 51:6**

Appearances can be deceiving. And let's face it; discovering someone is not the person we thought they were diminishes our ability to trust. That becomes a problem for Jesus when trusting Him serves as the foundation for our salvation. No wonder He takes authenticity so seriously.

Consider Jesus' words to the Pharisees, the highly respected religious leaders of his day who considered themselves extremely righteous.

> *"Woe to you, teachers of the law and Pharisees, you hypocrites!*
> *You are like whitewashed tombs, which look beautiful on the outside but*
> *on the inside are full of dead men's bones and everything unclean. In the*
> *same way, on the outside you appear to people as righteous but*
> *on the inside you are full of hypocrisy and wickedness.*
> **Matthew 23:27-28**

Jesus despises deception. When we deceive, we reflect the character of His enemy—the father of lies—instead of His own. John 14:6 teaches that Jesus is the truth. He wants us to reflect His character, not by acting like Him, but by *becoming* like Him on the inside.

How do you become like Jesus? By spending time in His presence and praying what David prayed in **Psalm 139:23-24**.

> *Search me, O God, and know my heart; test me and know my*
> *anxious thoughts. See if there is any offensive way in me,*
> *and lead me in the way everlasting.*

When you invite God to show you the truth of what dwells within your heart, you set yourself on the path to freedom.

"Then you will know the truth, and the truth will set you free."
John 8:32

Pray David's words from Psalm 139:23-24, opening your heart to revelation from God. Write what the Lord reveals on the lines below. Ask Him to help you release those things, that you might be an authentic reflection of Jesus' character.

_____

_____

_____

_____

_____

_____

_____

_____

_____

_____

_____

_____

_____

_____

_____

_____

_____

_____

Day 21: The Unfamiliar Path

> "I will lead the blind by ways they have not known, along unfamiliar
> paths I will guide them; I will turn the darkness into light before them
> and make the rough places smooth. These are the things I will do; I will
> not forsake them." Isaiah 42:16

We fear what we don't understand. And we often avoid what we fear.

Consider the abused woman who chooses to remain with her abuser. She
suffers at great cost, yet still she stays. She cannot conceive how she can
manage on her own. So she chooses familiarity over uncertainty.

Jesus seeks to guide you down an unfamiliar path. He has come to
empower each of us to leave our dark burdens and step into the light of
freedom. But like the abused woman who is too afraid to change her
circumstances, we often fight Him due to our fear. We prefer the comfort
of the familiar to the uncertainty of a new path.

Have you imprisoned yourself within the boundaries of the familiar? We
serve a God who specializes in surpassing what we can conceive (1
Corinthians 2:9). If you confine yourself to what's familiar, you'll miss
the bounty of His blessing.

Are you ready to exchange the ordinary for the extraordinary? Don't
limit yourself by embracing what feels natural. Choose the unfamiliar
path, the one marked by the presence of your Savior. There He will
enlighten you, guide you, and equip you. And you will soar.

*What's keeping you from the path God has set for you? Ask God to
reveal your fears and confess them on the lines below. Petition Him to*

help you trust Him for His best for you. Commit to remain with Him, as He has promised to remain with you.

_____

_____

_____

_____

_____

_____

_____

_____

_____

_____

_____

_____

_____

_____

_____

_____

_____

_____

_____

_____

Day 22: Take a New Step

"I will give you every place where you set your foot,
as I promised Moses." **Joshua 1:3**

God's Word overflows with promises. God stands ready to release His power. Blessings wait for His children to claim them.

Have you received those blessings? Does your life testify to God's faithfulness? God has promised to give you every place you set your foot. He means it, dear one.

"What I have said, that will I bring about; what I have planned, that will I do." **Isaiah 46:11**

God doesn't make empty promises. He has marked out a land of blessing for you to possess. But here's the tricky part. You will have to take a step of obedience to claim every piece of new ground.

That may not be what you wanted to hear. After all, most of us would prefer to have our blessings handed to us. We just want to see God move without having to exercise any effort. We'd certainly like to remove obedience from the equation. We'd rather do things our way.

But God's blessings flow into our lives as a result of faith. And we only *express* faith when we obey Him.

Obedience isn't a shackle, beloved. Obedience releases you from the constraints of your present circumstances and ushers you into God's blessing. Every step of faith you take in obedience to Christ increases your inheritance. Each time you trust Him, you gain ground. *And the enemy loses it.* It's time for you to claim your land.

Have you allowed God to demonstrate His faithfulness in your life? Ask God to reveal an area where you have withheld obedience, and write it on the lines below. Spend some time with Him in confession and commit to take a fresh step of faith as He leads you.

_____

_____

_____

_____

_____

_____

_____

_____

_____

_____

_____

_____

_____

_____

_____

_____

_____

Day 23: Out on the Water

"Come," he said. Then Peter got down out of the boat,
walked on the water and came toward Jesus.

Matthew 14:29

I love Peter. He wasn't one who played it safe, except, of course, for that fateful night when he heard the rooster crow.

With the exception of denying our Lord at His arrest, Peter is probably most known for his brief trek upon the surface of the water. He alone held the privilege of experiencing that miracle. But then again, no one else got out of the boat.

Peter's stroll on the lake has ignited many faith-filled believers into action over the centuries. Citing his example, eager disciples leap from their safe circumstances and plunge into the water to trust God for their miracle just like Peter did. They don't always have the outcome they expect.

We often miss a vital part of Peter's story, an action he took that we commonly overlook. Before Peter took one step out on that water, he asked Jesus to command him to.

"Lord, if it's you," Peter replied, *"tell me to come to you on the water."*
Matthew 14:28

Jesus responded with one word, *"Come,"* signaling to Peter that his journey upon the water was within His will.

Peter didn't just leap in faith hoping Christ would catch him. He first sought the Lord's permission. Then he stepped out in faith in direct obedience to Jesus' command.

Do you expect great things of God? Are you, like Peter, ready to get out of the boat and walk on water? Quiet yourself before God and ask Him to reveal His will to you, writing your thoughts on the lines below. Ask for the faith to step out in obedience and experience glory.

_____

_____

_____

_____

_____

_____

_____

_____

_____

_____

_____

_____

_____

_____

_____

_____

Day 24: Blessing in God's Will

> "If anyone chooses to do God's will, he will find out whether my teaching comes from God or whether I speak on my own."
> ### John 7:17

For generations, God has held out the promise to His people that He will bless them as they live out His will. The Israelites gladly received His promise and pledged to follow wholeheartedly. They stood at the base of Mt. Sinai after God's deliverance from Egypt, and responded with one voice,

> *"Everything the LORD has said we will do."*
> **Exodus 24:3**

Within weeks they were worshiping a golden calf and 3000 people died by the sword as a result of God's wrath.

Then God commanded the people to take possession of their land. In fear, they opted not to claim it, and an entire generation of Israelites missed the blessing of the Promised Land. They exchanged the land of milk and honey for 40 years of wandering in the desert. That's where they died.

All of them, that is, except for two men: Caleb and Joshua. Two chose to believe God's promises, and those two became the only recipients of God's blessing in their generation. But they didn't just receive the blessing; they also witnessed the miraculous. Their eyes saw the walls around Jericho crumble to the ground in response to mere marching and trumpet blasts. They experienced first hand the profound blessing of obedient trust.

Jesus came to empower each of us to live out His Father's will. He offers a challenge in John 7:17. Choose to trust His instruction, and you will *know* without doubt that He came from God.

Have you committed to follow Jesus wholeheartedly? Do you experience the blessings that flow from choosing His will? Ask God to reveal where you've made empty promises and offer a prayer of confession. Commit afresh to daily choose His will.

_____

_____

_____

_____

_____

_____

_____

_____

_____

_____

_____

_____

_____

_____

_____

_____

_____

_____

Day 25: Ask, Seek, Knock

"Ask and it will be given to you; seek and you will find; knock and the door will be opened to you."

Matthew 7:7

Imagine a treasure hidden from view along a well-traveled path. While its value is easily recognized when one stops to look, wanderers passing by can't glimpse it without effort. A traveler must seek it in order to discover it.

God's will is like that treasure hidden along the path. It holds great value and is easily found by one who searches for it, but one who neglects to look will never encounter it.

Do you pursue God's will – His desires, plans and goals – as you would seek a treasure? Or do you simply wander along life's path hoping to stumble upon it? If you wait for it to find you, dear one, you will likely miss it.

To experience the flow of God's blessing on your life, His will must be the focus of your journey. In it you will find protection and safety from the enemy's schemes. You will also encounter your purpose and experience His provision and power equipping you to fulfill it.

To discover God's will, He requires one thing of you. *Ask.* God isn't hiding His will; He simply asks that we seek it. And when we do, He promises to reveal it.

If any of you lacks wisdom, he should ask God, who gives generously to all without finding fault, and it will be given to him. **James 1:5**

God desires to reveal His will to you. You don't have to trust my word. Trust His.

Is the course of your path marked by God's will or your own? Do you pause long enough to listen for it? Ask God to reveal any area where you have stepped out of His will. Write down what He reveals and offer Him a time of confession. Ask Him to guide you into His perfect plan for you.

_____

_____

_____

_____

_____

_____

_____

_____

_____

_____

_____

_____

_____

_____

_____

_____

_____

_____

_____

Day 26: Thy Will Be Done

"Father, if you are willing, take this cup from me; yet not my will, but yours be done." Luke 22:42

Choosing God's will isn't always easy. You may believe with everything in you that God is good, trustworthy and true, but when a challenge arises and a difficult choice intersects your path, your flesh will scream with all it's might for you to run the other way. And you will want to.

It might comfort you to know you're not alone. Jesus Himself wrestled with His will while bound within the confines of His human flesh. Though He was perfect and without sin, the same battle raged within His heart that ravages yours.

When the time came for the cross to intersect His path, the Word made flesh didn't want it.

Have you considered that truth, dear one? Within the weakening limitations of His human form, Jesus wanted to escape God's will. Hear the agony in His words to His Disciples on the night of His arrest,

"My soul is overwhelmed with sorrow to the point of death."
Matthew 26:38

Who knows the goodness of God better than Jesus? Yet even He wrestled when obedience came at a cost.

Take heart in this truth, beloved. Your desire to run from God's will isn't sin. It's part of your human nature. You sin when you choose to obey that desire instead of trusting God.

Before you flee when God's revealed will seems too difficult, do what Jesus did. Pray. Draw on His strength to equip you to do what you don't want to do. Like Jesus, your obedience will result in glory!

Do you struggle with obeying God's will even though you believe He is for you? Does a difficult choice rob your peace even now? Write down the source of your fear and confess it to the Lord. Ask Him to help you overcome your human desires and surrender. Then get ready for glory!

_____

_____

_____

_____

_____

_____

_____

_____

_____

_____

_____

_____

_____

_____

_____

_____

_____

Day 27: Renown and Glory

Yes, LORD, walking in the way of your laws, we wait for you; your name and renown are the desire of our hearts. Isaiah 26:8

Centuries ago, a young shepherd boy felled a nine foot giant wearing full battle armor with only a sling and a stone. An entire army watched from the sidelines.

What would compel a boy to take such action while the fighting men around him trembled in fear? The giant defiantly taunted God's people for forty days while the army did nothing, believing Goliath had the power to defeat them. David's heart burned with anger that God's own army would allow such disgrace to come upon His name.

David asked the men standing near him, "What will be done for the man who kills this Philistine and removes this disgrace from Israel? Who is this uncircumcised Philistine that he should defy the armies of the living God?" **1 Samuel 17:26**

Glory drove David to action, but He wasn't after his own. His heart yearned to exalt the name of His God. So God used a willing warrior child to slay a giant, gloriously revealing His power before the watching eyes of two warring nations. Then He took that humble shepherd boy and made him a king.

We spend our lives seeking glory, fixed on exalting our own names. But occasionally, an individual comes along whose heart knows the great worth of our Lord and makes a different choice. Unlike the vast crowds who remain immobilized by self–absorption, this soul acts for the Lord's renown. And a marvelously surprising thing happens. He encounters the miraculous and finds himself basking in the glory he sought for the Lord.

> *"For whoever exalts himself will be humbled, and whoever humbles himself will be exalted."* **Matthew 23:12**

Whose glory do you seek, dear one? Do you remain on the sidelines preoccupied by your own circumstances or do you act for the Lord's renown? Ask God to search your heart and write what He reveals below. Pray for God to raise up warriors who will fight beside you for His glory.

_____

_____

_____

_____

_____

_____

_____

_____

_____

_____

_____

_____

_____

_____

Day 28: Zealous Adoration

The LORD your God has chosen you out of all the peoples on the
face of the earth to be his people, his treasured possession.

Deuteronomy 7:6

My dog adores me. Driven by her desire to be wherever I am, her greatest punishment is separation from me. She will immediately rouse herself from slumber to follow if I leave the room. And if she senses I'm not happy with her behavior, she instantly tries to remedy my displeasure.

She will tentatively approach me, laying her head down in humble submission, begging forgiveness. And of course I grant it, affectionately stroking her head to reassure her of my love. How could a loving owner not be moved by such blatant devotion?

I often think of how God must respond when His treasured possession reacts to His presence that way. How He must delight when His children long to be with Him and eagerly rise to follow Him. How joy must fill Him when a wayward child offers Him a sincerely repentant heart.

Unfortunately, I believe we more readily tend to imitate my dog's other prominent behavior. She tries to anticipate where I'm headed and rushes to get there first.

She loves to accompany me when I swim laps in the pool. Only she doesn't join me in the water, keeping pace with me. She races along the edge with one clear objective: to beat me to my destination.

She will pause momentarily at one end of the pool, just long enough to gauge where I'm headed. Then she runs to the other side and waits there to greet me. Occasionally, she moves so quickly she loses her footing and falls in. After swimming swiftly to the stairs, she climbs out to begin again. Eventually she collapses, exhausted.

Do your efforts to please God cause you to run ahead of Him? Are you so busy trying to guess where He's headed that you miss joining Him where He is? Ask God to help you discern where you've been marking your own path instead of keeping pace with Him. Commit to draw near to Him and remain wherever He is.

Day 29: A God who Prospers

"For I know the plans I have for you," declares the Lord,
"plans to prosper you and not to harm you, plans to give you
hope and a future." **Jeremiah 29:11**

You probably recognize this often quoted verse from Jeremiah. It serves as a foundational truth on which we rest our faith. *I can trust God because He is for me.*

This verse reveals an absolute truth you can depend on. When you trust God's plan and relinquish your own, you will discover the incomparable riches that flow from our redeeming God. And the beauty of what you experience will overwhelm you with gratitude.

But perhaps you've not yet recognized the other powerful truth revealed in this verse. The *you* that God addresses in this passage is plural.

At first that distinction may seem of little consequence, but consider the recipient to whom God speaks. The plural *you* changes the individual promise to a corporate one. Instead of a personal blessing for one, it becomes a collective or shared blessing for the whole.

What does that mean for you? Your individual blessing is directly tied to God's blessing for His people. You cannot fully live out and experience your personal blessing apart from God's plans to bless His church. You will prosper personally as you participate in God's efforts to prosper His kingdom as a whole.

Are you seeking your personal blessing from God or does your heart beat with Christ's, longing for the prosperity of His church? Ask Him to reveal where your heart truly lies and confess what He shows you on the lines below. Ask Him to align your heart with His, and offer Him your heart to be changed.

Day 30: Indispensable Member

Now you are the body of Christ, and each one of you is
a part of it. 1 Corinthians 12:27

The human body is amazing. Millions of distinct cells operate together in one fluid community to sustain life and generate movement. On its own, any particular cell doesn't offer much. But within the community of cells, each one reveals its value, working in its necessary role to maintain the health and prosperity of the whole.

Scripture compares the working of the church to the working of our physical bodies. Each body part holds necessary and equal value, with the exception of the head. Jesus,

. . . is the head of the body, the church . . . so that in everything
he might have the supremacy.
Colossians 1:18

Consider how our bodies function. The head governs the actions of each body part. A foot can't take a step without receiving a message from the brain to move. Fingers can't grasp an object without receiving a directive to do so. Even our ability to chew and swallow relies on communication from the brain to allow it.

Any part of the body that doesn't respond to the brain's instruction properly will not function as it should. As it falters, the entire body will suffer.

God designed the body of Christ—His church—to take action in response to His commands. Communication flows from Jesus, our head, through our central nervous system, the Holy Spirit. Only as each part properly responds to His instruction can the body fully operate and prosper.

Have you found your place in Christ's body? Are you looking to the church to meet your needs, or do you allow Jesus to direct you into your vital roles? Ask God to reveal any area where you may be ignoring His direction. Commit to participate fully in His glorious plan for His church.

_____

_____

_____

_____

_____

_____

_____

_____

_____

_____

_____

_____

_____

_____

_____

_____

Day 31: Not To Be Served

"For even the Son of Man did not come to be served, but to serve,
and to give his life as a ransom for many."

Mark 10:45

The church exists to serve. You probably selected your congregation by how well you believe it meets your needs. Maybe you enjoy the fellowship or the warm greetings you receive on Sunday mornings. Or, you like that the body is large and you feel you can slip in unnoticed. Perhaps the pastor's messages draw you here. You find Him clear and easy to understand . . . or you like that He usually gets you out on time.

You will judge a church by how well you believe it serves its people. As long as you perceive the church is meeting your needs, you'll consider it a good place to worship. Perhaps you haven't considered this fundamental truth. *You are the church.*

Most of us identify the church as a place to be served . . . a place for teaching, a safe haven to bring your prayer needs, a place to find help when you need it. But the church isn't a place, dear one. It's a body—Christ's body—every individual a member through whom Jesus serves the broken.

We are therefore Christ's ambassadors, as though God were making
his appeal through us. **2 Corinthians 5:20**

The church is not a building. It's a community of believers, serving one another and extending themselves to the lost. They are humble servants, choosing to empty themselves of their rights just as Jesus did, and making themselves available to serve others as He leads them.

Are you a part of the true church, beloved?

Do you believe the church exists to serve you, or do you recognize Jesus' call to serve through it? Ask God to show you the true desires of your heart. Pray for Him to unite your heart with His that you might become an ambassador of glory.

_____

_____

_____

_____

_____

_____

_____

_____

_____

_____

_____

_____

_____

_____

_____

_____

_____

_____

_____

Day 32: The Power of a Name

"And I tell you that you are Peter, and on this rock I will build my church, and the gates of Hades will not overcome it."

Matthew 16:18

Perhaps you wonder why God would ever choose to use the likes of you. When you gaze at your reflection in the mirror, you don't just see your face peering back at you. You see your history.

You know the restless doubt that robs your sleep, displaying itself in dark circles beneath your eyes. You see your failures. You see a stumbling sinner.

You imagine that's what God sees.

You're right, of course. Our omniscient God sees both your past and present struggles. But that's not what He sets His gaze upon. He chooses to see you in light of your potential. Then He intersects your path to offer you a fresh start.

At Peter's very first encounter with Jesus,

> *Jesus looked at him and said, "You are Simon son of John. You will be called Cephas" (which, when translated, is Peter).* **John 1:42**

Do you know what Peter means, dear one? *Rock.* Consider what that represents . . . strong . . . immovable . . . firm.

Rock is an interesting choice for the Disciple who would boldly pronounce Jesus to be the Christ and then turn around and deny Him.

Yet Jesus did not define Peter by his shortcomings or his failures. He spoke into his life what He desired him to be, and that's what Peter eventually became.

Have you allowed Jesus to raise you to your potential? Or do you use your mistakes to remain on the sidelines? Ask God to show you how His view of you differs from yours. Invite Him to help you believe in His vision of you.

_____

_____

_____

_____

_____

_____

_____

_____

_____

_____

_____

_____

_____

_____

_____

_____

Day 33: Doing Good Works

For we are God's workmanship, created in Christ Jesus to do good works, which God prepared in advance for us to do.

Ephesians 2:10

You were made for something great, and your soul longs to accomplish what you were made for.

Have you ever wondered why you never seem to remain satisfied? Why you set your heart on goal after goal, believing each will provide the contentment you seek, only to discover your joy in achieving them is fleeting? Somehow the longing lingers.

So you keep searching for the thing that will quiet the yearning.

You won't find it on your own. Christ provides the only source of true contentment.

For he himself is our peace . . . **Ephesians 2:14**

Yet even some of us who cling to Jesus find contentment elusive. We plod through life without ever tasting the satisfaction described in the Psalms.

You open your hand and satisfy the desires of every living thing.
Psalm 145:16

Why do so many who claim salvation through Christ remain unsatisfied? What have we missed?

Perhaps we miss out on the blessings available to us in Jesus because we neglect to follow Him. Instead, we take the lead in our own lives and strive to satisfy our own desires.

Here's the problem with that thinking: God created you to accomplish works that He prepared in advance for you to do. Your soul will never be satisfied until you do what you were made for, and Jesus offers the only path to get there.

Who has the lead in your life, dear one? Do you follow Jesus, or do you expect Him to follow and bless you? Ask Him to reveal what lies unsatisfied within you and lead you on the path toward its completion. Commit to follow wherever He leads.

_____

_____

_____

_____

_____

_____

_____

_____

_____

_____

_____

_____

_____

Day 34: No Right to Judge

"Why do you look at the speck of sawdust in your brother's eye and pay no attention to the plank in your own eye?

Matthew 7:3

God has called us to live in community. That means we need to live with each other.

That can be difficult to do when we allow judgment to filter into our relationships. Judgment tears down and destroys. It interferes with unity and quenches God's Spirit. Why? Because none of us are in any position to judge.

Even David, King of Israel, who God Himself described as *"a man after my own heart"* (Acts 13:22) proved himself unworthy to judge another man's actions. **2 Samuel 12:5** reveals David's reaction to hearing that a rich man took something that didn't belong to him.

David burned with anger against the man and said to Nathan, "As surely as the Lord lives, the man who did this deserves to die!

Nathan responded to David with these horrifying words,

"You are the man!" (**Verse 7**)

We so easily recognize sin in the life of another, yet we're often blind to its presence in our own.

To fellowship in harmony within the church, we can't focus our attention on the shortcomings we see in others. Instead, we must ask God to shift our gaze to our own. Removing ungodly behavior from the presence of the body begins with a look in the mirror. We can't change anyone else, but we can allow God to change us.

Do you have a tendency to be critical of others? Ask God to reveal any judgment you've been passing over someone else and confess it to Him. Invite God to show you any sin He wants to sift out of your life, and write what He reveals on the lines below. Then ask Him to help you renounce it and set you free!

_____

_____

_____

_____

_____

_____

_____

_____

_____

_____

_____

_____

_____

_____

_____

_____

Day 35: They Will be One

"I pray also for those who will believe in me . . . that all of them may be one, Father, just as you are in me and I am in you."

John 17:21-22

Jesus' last act on earth before His arrest and crucifixion was to kneel before the Father in prayer. Do you know who He prayed for, dear one? He prayed for you.

He didn't petition the Father to give you a prosperous life. He didn't request an easy journey and peaceful contentment. He asked that you become one with every other member of His body.

Consider the absurd limitations of that request in our natural world. Many families can't even agree on what TV program they should watch. And yet Jesus asked that all who would believe in Him would become one, just as He and the Father are one. *Same heart . . . same mind . . . same purpose . . . same Spirit.*

What outcome will such unity bring? I'll let Jesus answer.

"May they be brought to complete unity to let the world know that you sent me and have loved them . . ."
John 17:23

James 4:1 teaches that quarrels erupt among men when they follow their own selfish desires. Imagine the implications of thousands of God's children laying aside their own personal desires and allowing Jesus to unite their souls with His. Envision the power of a people who cease quenching the movement of God's Spirit and willingly surrender to His

74

authority. The day is coming, dear one. Jesus **always** gets what He prays for.

Will you be one of them? Will you willingly choose to set aside your preferences and desires so that Jesus can reveal His divinity through you?

Quiet your heart before God and ask Him to reveal any selfish desires keeping you from unity. Write what He reveals and relinquish them to Him. Ask Jesus to change your heart so that you may be one with Him and His body.

_____

_____

_____

_____

_____

_____

_____

_____

_____

_____

_____

_____

_____

_____

_____

Day 36: Blessed Community

*All the believers were one in heart and mind. No one claimed that
any of his possessions was his own, but they shared
everything they had.* **Acts 4:32**

If you were to visit a pre-school toddler room to observe the interaction between the children at play, you would often hear this word rising above the commotion. *Mine.*

Mine isn't a word children need to be taught. It enters their vocabulary instinctively, human nature driving them early on to fight to protect what's theirs. That nature compelling their possessive tirade is the same one that unceasingly seeks to exalt self—their sin nature, the very nature Jesus died to redeem.

Paul wrote some interesting words to the Corinthian church in **1 Corinthians 3:1**.

Brothers, I could not address you as spiritual but as worldly—mere infants in Christ.

What compelled Paul to describe these church members as infants?

You are still worldly. For since there is jealousy and quarreling among you, are you not worldly? Are you not acting like mere men? **(verse 3)**

There is nothing *merely* human about a believer housing the Spirit of the Living God. Perfect love and selflessness dwell within that soul seeking revelation through unity.

Though young in its existence, the Acts church described in our opening verse had left spiritual infancy and become mature; they no longer behaved as *mere men*. Instead, they allowed God's Spirit to fill and subdue them. Unlike their quarreling Corinthian brethren, their choice resulted in *"glad and sincere hearts, . . . And the Lord added to their number daily those who were being saved."* (**Acts 2:46-47**)

Would Paul describe you as worldly or spiritual? Ask God to help you gauge your own level of spiritual maturity and journal what He shows you. Pray for His Spirit to fill and mature you so you can become one with Him and His body.

_____

_____

_____

_____

_____

_____

_____

_____

_____

_____

_____

_____

Day 37: Give God the First

> In the course of time Cain brought some of the fruits of the soil
> as an offering to the Lord. **Genesis 4:3**

Have you ever wondered what made Cain's offering unacceptable to God? For years, I felt like he didn't get a fair shake. After all, Cain was the gardener. An offering from his crop should have delighted the Lord. He didn't even have a lamb to give!

Then God showed me the reason for His displeasure. It had nothing to do with the fact that Cain's offering came from the land. No, God's anger aroused when Cain didn't give Him his first.

After some time had passed, Cain brought *some* of his crop to present to the Lord. Cain didn't bring God his *firstfruits* (Exodus 23:19). He waited until he was satisfied he had enough for himself.

> *But Abel brought fat portions from some of the **firstborn** of his flock.*
> *The Lord looked with favor on Abel and his offering,*
> *but on Cain and his offering he did not . . .*
> **(Verses 4-5)**

Can you see why Abel's offering so delighted God, dear one? Abel brought the best of his firstborn lambs to present to the Lord; in doing so, he trusted that God would provide more.

Abel had no guarantee that his sheep would produce more lambs. Yet in reverence to God, He honored Him by giving Him his first . . . the *best* of the first. And God looked upon Abel with favor; then He blessed him with more.

78

In what areas of your life do you neglect to put God first? Your time? Your gifts? Your finances? Are you missing the blessing that comes from trusting Him? Ask God to reveal where you prioritize other things and write them below. How does He want you to start putting Him first? Offer a prayer of commitment to place Him where He deserves.

_____

_____

_____

_____

_____

_____

_____

_____

_____

_____

_____

_____

_____

_____

_____

_____

_____

_____

Day 38: Unwanted Offerings

"Oh, that one of you would shut the temple doors, so that you would not light useless fires on my altar! I am not pleased with you," says the Lord Almighty, "and I will accept no offering from your hands.

Malachi 1:10

It's hard to imagine God choosing to shut the doors of a church rather than accept the offerings of its people. Yet that's exactly what God said He desired to do through the prophet Malachi.

What would kindle such a response from a loving and gracious God? Isn't God pleased by offerings and sacrifice? Won't God gladly receive *any* offering from His people?

God is far more concerned with the heart of the giver than the offering itself. Yes, God's people paraded their offerings into the temple and placed them upon the altar. But their hearts weren't in it. They kept the best for themselves and gave God the leftovers.

God asked for the first; they gave Him what remained. He asked for the unblemished; they gave Him the blind and the lame.

Can you see why their actions would wound God's heart? What they brought to Him revealed exactly what they thought He deserved.

God's displeasure was aroused by what the people withheld from Him, not by what they gave.

"Cursed is the cheat who has an acceptable male in his flock and vows to give it, but then sacrifices a blemished animal to the Lord."
Malachi 1:14

Consider that your giving reflects how much you value God. Do you believe He is worthy of your best or your leftovers? Ask God to show you what your offerings reveal to Him about your heart and write His response. Pray for Him to align your heart with His worth.

_____

_____

_____

_____

_____

_____

_____

_____

_____

_____

_____

_____

_____

_____

_____

_____

Day 39: Reaping Generously

Give generously to him and do so without a grudging heart;
then because of this the LORD your God will bless you in all your
work and in everything you put your hand to.

Deuteronomy 15:10

More than anything, God desires your heart. And not just a piece of it, mind you. He wants the whole thing.

*Love the Lord your God with **all your heart** and with **all your soul** and with **all your mind** and with **all your strength**.* **Mark 12:30**

Why should we hold nothing back from God? Simply put, we will receive from God in direct proportion to what we offer Him; He responds to the *faith* of His children.

The more we release our hearts to Him, the more we experience the fullness of His love. The more time we give Him, the more He'll bless the use of our time. As we offer our gifts to Him, His blessing will begin to flow through the work of our hands. That's the principle of generosity.

Remember this: Whoever sows sparingly will also reap sparingly, and whoever sows generously will also reap generously. **2 Corinthians 9:6**

Have you been withholding from God because deep within you struggle to believe He will really keep His promises? Behind church attendance and proper Christian responses, has your nagging doubt paralyzed you into a dead, stagnant faith?

What if you chose to allow God's perfect love to cast out your fear and determined to trust God for His best? Perhaps it's time to stand on what you claim to believe.

Do you believe that God is for you? Do believe He can be trusted with your heart, your time, even your finances? Ask Him to infuse your heart with faith and help you to trust Him for His promises. Quiet your heart and allow Him to show you what you've been withholding from Him that He desires you to offer Him today. Trust Him through your obedience, and watch Him keep His promise.

_____

_____

_____

_____

_____

_____

_____

_____

_____

_____

_____

_____

_____

_____

_____

_____

_____

Day 40: More Sheep in the Pen

> "I have other sheep that are not of this sheep pen. I must bring them also. They too will listen to my voice, and there shall be one flock and one shepherd." **John 10:16**

I am so grateful that our loving God pursues. If He did not, I would not belong to Him. Neither would you.

How did God intersect your path, dear one? What caused you to want to commit your life to a servant King? How did you know His was a love worth tasting?

I saw it in the lives of a few humble servants who had chosen the way of surrender. Occasionally I would hear fantastic stories, impossible to believe, yet undeniably declaring, "He is real." I saw a few individuals who desperately loved a God I couldn't begin to understand, and I saw them experience a joy I longed for.

It wasn't my "church" experience that sent me in search of this Savior; my encounters with true disciples drove me to Jesus. I witnessed transforming love in a few select people, and the touch of grace on their lives left its mark on mine.

Who does God desire to rescue through you, dear one?

> " . . . go and make disciples of all nations, baptizing them in the name of the Father and of the Son and of the Holy Spirit, and teaching them to obey everything I have commanded you. And surely I am with you always, to the very end of the age."
> **Matthew 28:19-20**

Jesus commissioned His followers to finish what He began: to *love* the broken, to *pursue* the lost, to *serve* the needy . . . to *proclaim* His gospel of redemption. He is not yet satisfied. He will not return to restore perfection until every member of His flock rests safely within the fold.

His sheep remain scattered across the earth, deceived and lost. Some live right here in your community. Their hearts yearn to come home, and their Shepherd calls to them. Will yours be the voice that Jesus speaks through? Will your hands provide the divine touch that alters their path?

Are you a true disciple of Jesus? How is He asking you to respond to Him? Answer Him. Pray for the rise of His church and commit to follow Jesus wherever He leads.

Are you ready to go deeper? Do you desire to start living God's plan for your life?

Tested by Fire will guide you into your eternal purpose.

This four week, interactive study will help you consider:

- Do you really know Jesus?
- Do you have the ability to hear from God?
- Are you building your life according to your plans or God's purpose?
- Are you wearily struggling to make something of your own life, or are you living evidence of God's power?

**How You Live Matters....
Leave a legacy that lasts!**

"Kelley's Bible study was truly a transforming experience. God's Word really comes alive in the pages of her book. It was the best study I have ever been a part of." ~ Carrie, Hanover, PA

"This study has been a confirmation, awareness, and revelation in my life about who Jesus is and what He wants from me. This helped answer some questions I have had lingering, afraid to ask." ~ Jen, North Bennington, VT

"*Tested By Fire*, has challenged me to look at my relationship with God and see whether I really love him the way He calls me to, whole-heartedly. Through this study I have rededicated my life to living for Him and seeking Him daily! I have drawn closer to God through this study and learned how to hear His voice. I know that following the Father's will for my life brings about a peace that can be found no where else." ~ Mindy, Hanover, PA

"I feel like God is trying to reveal Himself to me through it . . . saying, 'Look here. This is who I am.' I am very moved by it." ~ Kevin, St. Pete Beach, FL

"Kelley Latta provides an invaluable tool that will help open your eyes to God's truth. " ~ Lenwood, Montclair, NJ

"Each day I felt like the Master himself was teaching me directly! Some evenings I found myself hugging my book, like a child hugging his teacher at the end of the school day, eagerly waiting for the next day to come to hear what the Teacher had waiting for me to learn. Each day opened up to me who God was and what He wanted for me." ~ Miriam, Hanover, PA